Martha Glas

Woman's Work in the Church

Martha Glas

Woman's Work in the Church

ISBN/EAN: 9783742812537

Manufactured in Europe, USA, Canada, Australia, Japa

Cover: Foto ©ninafisch / pixelio.de

Manufactured and distributed by brebook publishing software
(www.brebook.com)

Martha Glas

Woman's Work in the Church

WOMAN'S WORK IN THE CHURCH.

BY

MRS. MARTHA TYLER GALE.

BOSTON:

CONGREGATIONAL PUBLISHING SOCIETY,

BEACON STREET.

BOSTON:

STEREOTYPED BY O. J. PETERS AND SON,

73 FEDERAL STREET.

TOPICS.

Woman's Work in the Church.

" Help those women who labored with me in the gospel."
Phil. iv. 3.

MORE than two-thirds of the members
of our churches are women. The Church
cannot possibly afford to allow this large
number to be idle. They should all be
enlisted for service.

We rejoice to believe that the order
of deaconesses will be revived ; but beside this it should be the aim of every
church and every pastor to engage the
whole sisterhood in church work, and
the effort of all others who have talent
for organizing, to divide and direct labor,
and persuade each one to do her part.

Many women have leisure, after all home duties are performed, which might be devoted to the Master's service. Some wealthy women are suffering in listless idleness, for want of satisfactory employment. It would be the greatest kindness to interest them in Christian labor.

But not only should ladies of leisure be engaged. It will be found that those who have already enjoyed the satisfaction there is in the full employment of all their powers, and the happiness of self-denying toil for the good of others, are usually ready to take up new work. Some one has said, "If you want to get a pair of shoes for a poor child, do not go to a rich, pampered, childless lady. She will say, 'The poor don't mind going barefoot: they get used to it.' Go to the hard-working mother of six little ones, and you will meet with a cordial response, 'You are right: the child must have shoes. I will do my best to help get them.'" So the industrious, who are already most occupied, are sometimes willing to assume fresh burdens, and prove the best church workers.

We found a lady hurried with embroidering and trimming. She showed us all the ornamentation she had commenced, saying, "I am as industrious as a bee." We could not admire it, for we knew it engrossed her mind. We viewed it with pain, and thought, How useless all! Her own countenance fell; then in excuse she said, "I do not know any poor people, or any to work for. I busy myself with this to while away my time."

Should a Christian woman live thus

consciously for self? Things of beauty, tasteful ornaments, are somewhat desirable; but is it right to spend so much of our time in purely selfish adornment? *Our time*, did we say? Is it our time? Who gives us our time, and for what purpose? Are *we* not bought with a price? If "she that liveth in pleasure is dead while she liveth," how is it with her who lives in busy idleness or in worthless, selfish industry?

O sisters! leave this childish play, which dwarfs the intellect, and belittles the soul, and come up to your high calling. Adorn yourselves, as "becometh women professing godliness, with good works." If you are so fond of your needles, use them more as did Dorcas. Leave the canvas "red with the blood of murdered time." God can give you richer garlands. Leave all undue ornamentation of person or of homes, and seek first to gain the "fine linen, clean and white, — the righteousness of saints;" that raiment which will ere long be transfigured, and become "glistering" as the sun, "white as the light."

While we write, voices of young ladies come to us, singing Lucy Larcom's hymn.

> "Heavenly Father, I would wear
> Angel garments white and fair;
> Angel vesture undefiled
> Wilt thou give unto thy child.
> Take the raiment soiled away,
> That I wear with shame to-day:
> Give my angel robes to me,
> White with heaven's own purity;
> Clothe me in my angel dress,
> Beautiful with holiness."

How appropriate this petition for maidens who cannot forget their attire!

But many will say, "We wish to be useful. We should prefer to work for the Church, did we know how. What can we do?"

Much every way. First, earnestly implore Christ to show you some work for him, and give you a heart to do it; and you may find both to-morrow. While we suggest some methods of work, others will doubtless occur to you.

PRAYER.

We can surely *all pray more.*

Without true prayer, all work is vain. Prayer is the life and soul of work, its inspiration, its wisdom, and its success. The one who prays most truly serves the Church best.

Now, woman seems appointed, like the Vestals of old, to guard the sacred fires on the altars of devotion. She is fitted by her sensitive nature and her more favorable circumstances for this hallowed work. The physical weakness and comparative helplessness of woman induces a sense of dependence upon God ; her responsibilities in the care of children often incite her to more prayerfulness ; while her opportunities for retirement and leisure devolve this sacred duty especially upon her. How guarded from ambition is she in the seclusion of her quiet home, how well protected from the currents of avarice and worldliness that sweep through the marts of greedy trade ! She is free from the anxieties of professional and business life which absorb the mind. It is far easier for her to keep herself unspotted from the world than for him who presses through the jostling crowd in the miry streets. The even tenor of her way lies so near the closet, she may at almost any time step within, and make her requests known to God.

The glory of this best of good works is that it can be done at all times, — in sickness or in health, at home or abroad, in the closet, in the sanctuary, and even by the way. The pure-hearted, believing girl may find it easier to gain access to God than the gifted statesman weary of the crooked ways of this perverse world, or the princely merchant distracted with pressing cares; and the aged and infirm sister, wondering why her useless life is lengthened, may be answered, " Christ delays his coming that you may still longer enrich the world by your intercessions." While the hands are chained to household toil, the heart may rise on the

wings of prayer ; and though to earn her
daily bread one is forced to stitch, stitch,
stitch, her sweet comfort may be to pray,
pray, pray.

We remember a woman, who, every
morning after her husband left for his
business, retired to pray that he might be
saved from covetousness, and especially
from unfairness in trade.

One told us, " My husband had been
sceptical ; at last he became unsuccessful in business. I was so anxious about
the support of our large family that I
cried to God in my distress, and implored
his pity and help. I could do nothing
besides ; for I was helplessly sick, and
shut up to prayer. I encouraged my
husband, and kept him from despair,
saying, 'I am pleading with God : wait
now, and see if he does not interpose

for us.' More than once he was so strangely and in such an unexpected manner relieved from his embarrassments, that he became convinced it was in answer to my prayers. Now the desire of my heart has been granted, and he rejoices in the same faith."

A maiden lady said, "I am continually praying for the neglected children I see in the city. Truly 'more are the children of the desolate than of the married woman, saith the Lord,' there are such hosts of them; and I plead for them all." How happy that this large-hearted woman could thus adopt the many so much in need of loving remembrance!

Another says, "Whenever my thoughts are at liberty, they turn to God, and almost always take the form of petition. I constantly single out individuals, and intercede for them; and I find that in course of time they are almost all converted. I am astonished at the willingness of God. I seem to gain so much of what I ask both of temporal and spiritual good!"

She was wise in being thus specific. There is great advantage in selecting particular persons, praying for them by name, and increasing our interest for them by dwelling upon their need of conversion, and on the service they may render to the cause of Christ.

Women such as these, though unnoticed and unknown, are the benefactors of the world and the strength of the Church. They are like the forces beneath the earth and in the air, unseen but powerful, which cause the garden of the Lord to bud and blossom, and fruits of righteousness to spring forth on every hand. The odors sweet which are the prayers of saints, the incense which rises from their heart's altars, descend in dew on the tender herb, or in the great rain of God's strength. In answer to their requests, all the common means of grace become effectual, and the impenitent are won. They plead for the divine spirit, and it is given.

PRAYER-MEETINGS.

Those who thus abide in Christ by constant prayer *carry a spiritual power to the social service.* Others watch for their coming, and miss them when absent. Though silent, they give courage and inspiration to those who speak. Their songs not only express their own devotion, but awaken the same emotions in those who listen. If the orator searches his audience for the interested hearer, and grows eloquent only when he meets a "listening eye," how much more does the preacher long for Christian sympathy from devout hearers, who wing his words with prayer ! "Do go with me," said a minister to a pious wife and sister. "Let me know that two are there praying for me, or I cannot preach." Where there are many earnestly importuning, the place becomes the house of God, the gate of heaven.

"Such ever bring Thee where they come."

Is it thus within our power to gain inestimable blessings for others; and shall we not rejoice to do this great work for the Church ?- The Lord seems to say *to us*, "*Prove me now*, and see if I will not pour you out a blessing."

If women are anxious to aid religious services, they will make all their arrangements so as to be present, and *will invite others to accompany them.* How often persons are absent, when wise planning would have prevented their being detained! Sometimes a woman will invite her friends, when every guest should be at the prayer - meeting. " I never thought," she pleads; but the man who forgot the sabbath confessed, " In that was my sin: it was my duty to remember." Will not the sensitive Saviour, who begged his friends to watch with him one hour, be wounded that they meet with you, and neglect the appointment he has made to be in the midst, where two or three are gathered in his name ?

A pastor lamented that, on his way to

his preparatory lecture, he saw three young ladies, all members of his church, out playing croquet.

Women desirous to assist the worship of others will be willing, for the time at least, to lay aside their most " costly array," and all conspicuously gay clothing, where the rich and the poor meet together. They may say, " I never give it a thought ; " but the weak sister behind them, with more ambition than ability to wear the same, may give it many thoughts, and possibly thoughts akin to envy. Paul would eat no meat while the world stood, if it made his weak brother to offend.

FEMALE PRAYER-MEETINGS.

Women may do the Church great service by *sustaining female meetings*. Many revivals have had their origin in women's prayer-meetings ; indeed, a church that has no such meetings can hardly expect to be greatly blessed. They should be not only for prayer and Christian conversation, but for consultation as to what can be done for Christ's cause. In some places the members go out and draw in the unconverted, that they may be influenced in the atmosphere of prayer. But there should be more careful preparation made for these meetings. The mere relation of personal experience will not long continue to edify. God's word should be searched ; we should dig deep into its mine of wealth, till we can bring up hidden treasures, then fuse them with our own heart's fire, with prayer, earnest thought, and constant practice, before we can become truly instructive.

We knew a teacher, a woman of thought and deep piety, who accomplished wonders for her scholars by an hour of prayer with them weekly. A devoted sabbath-school teacher persuaded her class of girls to meet her for prayer between the sabbaths, till all of them, catching her spirit, grew up heavenly-minded.

THE SABBATH SCHOOL.

Of course it is expected that every Christian who wishes to be useful will be in the sabbath school, unless other duties interfere; and that, while a teacher, she will do all in her power for her class to help them socially and in temporal things, to start them intellectually, and train them spiritually for usefulness.

A young man was long unsuccessfully seeking employment. His rich relatives left him to try, and try in vain, till his Sunday-school teacher, a poor young man, found him a situation.

"You first taught me to think; you showed me how to study," said a gifted scholar to her former sabbath-school teacher: "your influence and instructions educated me intellectually and religiously."

"How came *you*, situated as you were, to become a missionary?" we asked one who had proved very laborious and useful. "I owe it all to the sabbath-school teacher I had when I was a girl. She was untaught, except by God and his word, but was a missionary at home. She imbued me with her spirit."

And yet, sad to relate, another scholar

says, "I have been in a lady's class three years, and she does not seem to care the least for me. She has never so much as asked me whether I am a Christian."

ADVICE AND COUNSEL.

You may also instruct the ignorant by *kind, judicious counsel.* If God has given you more wisdom, is it not your duty, as far as consistent, to make it useful to others?

Some women were complaining of the great severity of a young mother near them, with her little girl. They said, " She means well enough, but don't know any better. She will ruin the child's disposition, if not her health." — " But why don't you call, and contrive kindly to advise her? Tell her how you lost your child, and how we reproach ourselves, when it is too late, for the least impatience or harshness with a child." — " Oh! we cannot: it might seem like meddlesome interference." So the ignorant mother took her abused child, and moved away unreproved. Was this right? " Thou shalt *in any wise* rebuke thy neighbor, and not suffer sin upon him."

You rejoice that the homelike and friendly cheer of your parlor attracts the young man from gayer haunts, and keeps him from temptations. You may be the one, in winning words, to " speak to that young man," if need be, to caution him, with the tenderness of a mother, or the gentleness of a sister. So of the young woman who has no mother near to guide her. " I may gain their ill-will," you object. What is that compared with a duty? You may secure their lifelong gratitude.

A young woman of our acquaintance heard that a promising young man was becoming intemperate, and her Christian sympathies were earnestly enlisted. "Does any one warn him?" she asked. "He is away from all his best friends. If I had but an introduction, I am sure I would expostulate with him, no matter how he may regard it." The next day she had an introduction, when she told him frankly what she had heard of his talents, and of his danger from stimulants, and begged him not to ruin himself, and blight all his fine prospects. Instead of offending him, as others predicted, she gained his respect and affection. He removed from his old evil associates, and took board in the same house with her for protection. It was not long before, proving himself worthy, he intrusted himself further to her care.

But this most difficult work of counsel, and especially of admonition, should only be undertaken after most earnest seeking of aid from the Spirit of wisdom.

TOWARDS SERVANTS.

It is presumed that you have proved yourselves to *be the sincere friend of every servant you employ*, even to your washer-woman, and that she confides in and relies upon you for help, counsel, and comfort in time of need.

If these are Romanists, you will not be so unwise as to attack the church they venerate, but rather congratulate them that they hold with you the supreme divinity of Christ, and the sacrificial atonement he made for our sins by his death. Then you will discreetly guard them against trusting in good works, in penance, in absolution, or in church sacraments, instead of in the merits of that death ; and against interposing Mary between their souls and their divine Saviour, the "one Mediator." Perhaps you may persuade them to read the narratives in the Douay Bible, especially the story of the dying thief, which so clearly teaches salvation by faith alone.

There are those who prove that the relation of mistress and maid may be the interchange of gratefully received kindnesses. A bright "Thank you," for any unexpected service or little attention, is as deserved by your servant as by your friend, and far more valued. "You are so constantly kind and obliging, we love you," said a lady to her girl. The surprised servant answered by tears. It was like the kiss of her mother, when she was in green Erin.

Do not say this is not church work. We send missionaries abroad for this purpose. True, good judgment is needed; but can it be doubted that the Church should aim to evangelize all the misguided among us, or that it will ere long arouse itself to perform this sadly neglected duty? Would every Christian woman instruct the *one or two* whom she can influence, how many might be taught, who may be the mothers of a new generation!

GIVING.

Women should *aid and promote benevolence.* It must be confessed, that owing

to their greater timidity and fear for the
future, and the narrowness of their usual
interests and occupations, women are
more penurious than men. Some wives
check the generosity of their husbands,
while others incite them to noble deeds.
The wife of John Howard was in full
sympathy with all his early philanthropy.
Finding a surplus in his purse at one
time, he proposed taking her on a pleas-
ure-trip to London. "What a pretty
cottage that sum would build!" she said.
So the journey was given up, and a poor
tenant's family made more happy. Many
ways will occur to you by which women
can swell the amount in the Lord's
treasury. The Woman's Board of Missions is surely worthy of encouragement
from every woman, though it be but by a
mite or a word.

A factory girl told us, " I found I was making a great deal of money, but I was growing mean and stingy ; and I resolved that I would force myself to give for religious objects. It was hard. I had a great battle with myself, but I determined that I would give a tenth of all I earned. Now I take a deal of comfort in it. It counts up remarkably. I have ten or twelve dollars for foreign missions, and five, seven, or eight, for the different home objects."

" The example must have been beneficial," we said. " Yes. It did a world of good, the collectors said. People asked, 'Who is this?' — ' She works in the mill, but she thinks it her duty to give,' they answered. After that, gentlemen and ladies were ashamed to put down a dollar or two beside ten from a factory girl."

"Alas! I cannot earn a cent!" exclaims some young lady. "I am obliged to ask father for all I have." But, if you ask for edgings and for jewelry, why not for Christ? Perhaps you could ask him to let you earn something to give. A father gave a daughter money to buy a shawl; she begged permission to buy a cheaper shawl, and give away what remained. In this way many might gain the great benefit of denying themselves for Christ. What will it matter by and by, whether the shawl be costly or not? while the sum saved may give a cup of cold water in remembrance of Him who was athirst for our sakes, or become like the precious ointment poured over the nail-pierced feet.

CONVERSATION.

Women should aim to *raise the tone of conversation* in society.

How proverbially small and profitless is the talk even when Christian women meet together! while without being strictly religious, conversation might always promote intelligence, piety, and kind feeling. Comments upon the faults of Christians cannot fail to injure the influence of the Church. If we must speak of others, let us tell of some noble activity, some excellence attained, some good accomplished, never fearing to change the subject when it degenerates. Mark the houses where conversation proves most profitable, and there make your most frequent calls ; and avoid the persons who cannot be lifted above scandal, gossip, or frivolous chit-chat. It is well after a visit to recall what has been said for future improvement; for those who succeed in leading conversation, and elevating its tone, usually make a study of topics to introduce, and choose well their words.

AMUSEMENTS.

Women can *plan suitable amusements*, and watch that they do not slide into what is over-exciting and excessive, or interfere with the interests of religion. Here they should be discerning and far-sighted, for in this way they may do great good or great harm.

We heard a neighboring minister lamenting, " I have felt impelled to make a great effort for our young people. I have strained every nerve, and devised

3

every way to interest them in religion; but there was no sympathy and no co-operation on the part of the church. Even pious mothers were taken up with planning amusements which diverted the attention of their children. The disappointment nearly crushed me." How was it these women did not discern the time?

Women can frown down that which is deteriorating, smile upon all that is improving, and often they have a persuasive grace to bring others to their views. To infuse a religious element into social intercourse, is a part of woman's work for the Church.

Boys are exposed to peculiar dangers. Wicked men are on the watch to ruin them, and the Church ought to be still more anxious and vigilant to save them.

Yet how often are they neglected by the good, and left to drift into evil till they are lost to the Church ! Young women will sometimes gain an influence over boys, and greatly aid the mother in guiding them toward a safe course in this forming period of their lives.[1]

RELIGIOUS BOOKS.

Good reading is a great safeguard to youth.

Whoever can induce one to read a thoroughly religious book does them a great service. Loaning and giving religious books that are attractive and interesting as well as instructive, of which

[1] We know two young ladies, sabbath-school teachers, who sustain a lyceum and reading-circle in their own parlors with most unselfish labor, for the sole purpose of keeping boys and girls from amusements that have proved injurious to them.

there are now so many, is one way of accomplishing good.

CHURCH VISITING.

Women may greatly aid church work by *religious visiting*.

A pastor, knowing that some new parishioners were sad and homesick, asked a woman to call on them, when she replied, "I have more acquaintances now than I can attend to. I cannot make more." She forgot the direction, "Love ye therefore the stranger." Visits of mere kindness, to make strangers more at home, may be church work. So of calls on those just coming into the church, to give them the right hand of welcome, and assure them of the friendly interest of the membership. Were every new member met with a hearty cordiality as if coming to a united brotherhood, and constantly encircled with loving sympathy, many might be saved from wandering.

Women should be especially attentive to the humble and retiring, and those liable to be overlooked, that they may not be discouraged and imbittered by imagining themselves despised by those in more influential positions. They have no right, you say, to grow suspicious, and presume upon the disdain of those in better circumstances. True, but how little painstaking might remove such prejudices! How small a return for superior advantage, to treat all who are less favored with consideration, at least those who attend the same church; to do a small kindness, make a short call, give a friendly greeting, even a pleasant smile or a nod as you pass! None but those who have been sadly depressed know how much these trifles sometimes lighten heavy hearts. A dejected woman has just now remarked in our hearing, " The poor want a kind word more than money." Do not stand upon ceremony, and wait with averted face for some third person to introduce you formally. It is the averted face that does the mischief. Break the ice by some kind inquiry, if you should both linger side by side at the church door, or chance to meet elsewhere. All know that success tends to foster self-esteem, and contempt of those who are unsuccessful. " Ye have despised the poor," remonstrates James with a church. The least lurking of contempt for the poor, the weak, and ignorant, is so far from

Christlike that it is a great sin, and may nullify the virtue of large charities.

SYMPATHY.

For religious visiting, as indeed for most Christian labor, the first qualification, after a fervent zeal for Christ, is a quick and *tender sympathy;* an immediate, warm, and deep interest in those to be benefited ; a power to place one's self in their circumstances, and enter into their feelings. All successful workers have these ready, ardent sympathies. The cold and unsympathetic seldom move or win others, while there are few so hard as not to be touched by an affectionate interest in their welfare.

There is a remarkable worker, who, as soon as he learns the character and circumstances of a person, seems at once

to love them almost as his kindred, and
to be as sincerely concerned for them as
though there were not another person in
the world. He gives his whole heart, as
it were, to whatever case comes before
him. A human soul wherever found is
precious to him beyond price, and he sets
himself to win it.

"I want," said a magnetic preacher,
"first to look over my audience, and take
them all into my heart." Oh! it is this
taking them into the heart, as Christ
takes us all into His great heart of pity
and of love, that is the secret of all
Christian magnetism and success.

We of the Church are finite. Our
hearts are small. We can each interest
ourselves deeply in but few at one time;
and this makes it important that each
member, women as well as men, the

aged and the young, should be searching out those whom they can take under their loving care, so that every individual within reach of the Church shall feel the power of a personal influence drawing them to Christ.

Now, woman, with her heritage of weakness and suffering, gains these quick sympathies. It is this, with the grace of God, that may give her the wisdom to direct, and the tact needed to approach others on personal and delicate themes; so that, with sufficient piety, women are often the best workers. Especially do feminine tenderness and refinement find their appropriate sphere in visiting the sick and afflicted, with whom bluntness or want of delicacy gives a fresh wound.

VISITING THE SICK.

By *visiting the sick*, we do not mean calling on those whose houses are thronged, and whose peace is disturbed by visits of inquiry and compliment; but searching out the obscure invalids who linger, lonely and forgotten, having few comforts and few friends, who sigh for some token of remembrance, and need something fresh to connect them with the outside world ; to whom the sight of a new face, the tones of a new voice, or any change, give relief to the wearying monotony of confinement.

If, as Hannah More says, "the care of the poor is the vocation of woman," how much more does all that is implied in *the care* of the sick poor devolve upon her! These visits should usually be short and cheery, either for ministry or to carry some comfort. At least, go with some good news. Be as sunshine in the darkened room. Few except hyponchondriacs desire condolence. They had better hear of some happiness, some success, although we should show sufferers that we appreciate their efforts to maintain self-control and cheerfulness. Assure them of the continual love and pity of God ; for afflictions sometimes seem to us judgments for our sins, rather than fatherly chastisements ; and convince them of the tender sympathy of Him who bore our sicknesses.

It may sometimes be better *to send* than *to go*, if you can teach an unpractised one, or show those unused to such work, the enjoyment there is in helping the helpless. All who wish to comfort

the sick would do well to read Florence
Nightingale's "Notes on Nursing," in
order to gain something of her wisdom,
and imbibe her spirit ; for her keen sympathies with all the suffering creatures
of God are an inspiration to every true-
hearted woman.

CALLING ON THE AFFLICTED.

What true sympathy should she possess who goes to *weep with those who
weep*, to carry to the sorrow-stricken the
rich consolations God has provided for
all the varied forms of grief ! It is her
work to point the bereaved to Him who
can fill every vacancy in the heart, and
satisfy every longing, and, in place of
our loved and lost, can give his own
sweet peace, — the one who calls himself a father an elder brother, a husband ;

and who promises to comfort as a "mother comforteth."

Does she visit the widow and the fatherless? How many expressions of God's peculiar regard for them, how many promises of especial protection, she can quote to them from the Scriptures!

Those who are infirm with age should never be neglected ; for, with the decline of vital force, there is often a painful sinking of courage. Such need to be reassured by the promises, "He will be our guide even unto death," "Even to your old age, and even to hoar hairs, will I carry you. I have made, and I will bear ; even I will carry, and will deliver you." It must be a pleasant duty to remind those who are nearing and are fearing the dark valley, of the rest that remaineth, and the mansions in the place prepared for them.

It is said that the death of a young child oftener proves a spiritual blessing than any other affliction. A woman said to me, "Besides my other great trials, I lost my first child. Then I was thoughtful: I longed for religion. If I could have gone to church, and been instructed, or had some Christian come to me and guided me, — taught me to submit my will to God's, — it might have saved all my long rebellion against him. Oh, how many weary years of wretched discontent, before I found comfort for all my sorrows, and peace of mind from Jesus!"

Invalids and convalescents are sometimes in this subdued and receptive state of mind; and Christian woman should be watching to guide all such, and to drop the precious seed when the soul is thus softened by tender grief.

RELIGIOUS CONVERSATION.

But more important and more neglected church work is *visiting for religious conversation.*

These visits should usually be merely
calls of friendship till confidence is won.

Many of us who are Christians need
constant rousing to duty, and those most
earnest may do much to quicken others.
They should win such praise as the
apostle gave: "Your zeal hath provoked
very many." "Exhort one another
daily" is the command. We knew a
woman confined to her bed for years,
who was a continual incentive to good
deeds, and a stimulating spiritual power
to all who knew her.

Some ladies in a city complained, "It
is so hard to raise money sufficient to

hire our Bible-readers and female visitors!" We asked, "Where are your
volunteer workers? In all your city
cannot women be found who wish to
labor for Christ, — women of leisure, or
partial leisure, who will take small, quiet
districts, say the nearest to their own
homes, and make themselves responsible
for the faithful visiting of that community?
Some laborers, strong and firm, of course
must be hired for the most difficult parts
of the work; but a great deal might be
done by your own ladies, if they would
undertake it; and the reflex influence on
the church would be blessed, much more
so than the mere giving of money. To
be sure, it would require self-denial, preparation for the work, the cultivation of
tact, tenderness and friendliness of manner; but all this can be soon gained, if

prayerfully sought; and it would be sought and gained, did Christian women but know what a rich reward Christ gives to all who labor directly for him."

But they say, "We are not adapted to this: it is better for us to give; we prefer to give." They are somewhat like the man who said, "I cannot pray: I am not used to it; I don't know how. I will pay somebody to pray." Ladies have learned to work for Christ in this way, and ladies who have been trained, and have expected, to be the most exclusive. This exclusiveness is not of Christ, but of the world. Why should we not sometimes leave "our set," and go out, like the Good Samaritan, to find who is our neighbor? If in the city, go as a missionary, frankly confessing your errand. If in the country, go as a friend.

4

How much more satisfactory than calling on the "dear five hundred friends " it must be, to know that you are befriending those who need friends, are pleasing Christ, and perhaps are winning grateful love !

There is a pious girl in the city of ——, only fifteen years of age, who has "her poor family," which she visits frequently, and assists in many ways. There is no waste in her home : Lucy wants it for "her poor family." She is almost worshipped by them. The delight of the children at her approach is worth more to her than rubies and pearls.

It cannot lower one of high position thus to "condescend to men of low estate." Did it lower Agnes Jones, rich and learned, to go out on her father's large estate, and nurse paupers, and die at last from over care and work in the Liverpool almshouse? or did it degrade the gifted Mrs. Judson to do this work in foreign lands? It raised them nearer the dignity of the ministering spirits, and of the condescending One who went about doing good.

How were the women employed who will be held in everlasting remembrance because they labored with Paul in the gospel? They must have visited for religious conversation, calling first upon one woman, and then on another, telling of Jesus, and persuading them to become his disciples.

We have now in mind honorable women, wealthy and cultivated, who rejoice to do this work for the church. They visit not only the very poor, and their own social circle, but the industrial classes; those who are not rich, but yet are tenacious of their independence.

This is important in the country, where there are no hired visitors, and where jealousies between the different classes often prevent kind feeling, and hinder the progress of religion. A distinguished woman has remarked, "I would like to know my neighbor in the palace : I must know my neighbor in the cottage." This is attended with difficulties, and ladies will object, "We wish to be friendly, but the social barrier is between us: how are we to surmount it? The pride and reserve and reluctance are on the other side. They do not wish to have us call." Hints to the wise are sufficient.

One lady in a village made her way by borrowing. The large house overlooked the small garden of the cottage,

She had wished to call; she longed to do these neighbors good, and she knew it was her duty to attempt it; but she was made aware that she would not be welcome. One day she put on a plain dress and a sunbonnet, and ran over, saying, "I have come to ask a favor. My soup needs an onion. I see you have them in your pretty garden. May I beg one? How bright your flowers are!" &c. Another time she went to beg nasturtions for her bouquet. Favors asked could be returned, and she could sit and chat. Jealous prejudices were removed. "Why, she is not proud, as I thought when I saw her riding round in her carriage!" After a time, she could tell what a comfort her religion had been to her, how little worth the living life would be without the hope in

Christ, how she longed to have all possess it. At last, her genuine regard was so undoubted, that she could plead, "I cannot bear to have you neglect this matter : you must be a Christian."

Another broke the ice by saying, "I have the old-fashioned country way : I want to know all my neighbors. In case of sickness or accident I might need their help, or they might need mine. I want them to feel free to call on me if I can help them." Of course she was soon regarded as a friend. How could her friendship be doubted? She gave bright apples and pictures to the children, and in the twilight knit socks for the baby. Was not this as well as to make presents to the pampered children of the rich? She could present the claims of Christ, even urge them.

Still another learned that the mechanic's wife, not far from her house, was sick without a nurse. The lady went over, and spent an hour or two every morning nursing her, for a fortnight. While giving her her broth, she told her how Christ made all her own bed for her in her last sickness, how ready he was to meet all seekers. When the sick one recovered, her kind nurse found she had won a heart: soon she had won a soul.

Begin with the lowest, was Howard's rule ; that is, seek out the most suffering, most needy, first : but do not cease your efforts here. How many laborers do this! How few have courage to exhort the opulent and self-complacent! How few venture to warn the haughty brethren of Dives! It should be one who frequents their dwellings, of the same refinement; one who speaks tenderly, wisely, and well. May it not be the cultured lady or the maiden of address who always wins her way, and can say whatever she pleases? Ah, if Salome, who pleased Herod so well, had but appealed to his better nature, he might have heard John again, and have done many more things gladly, things that accompany salvation. Had she possessed the spirit of the little captive maid who saved Naaman, possibly she, too, might have had the star of a ruler in her crown of glory. " The tender and delicate woman among you, who would not adventure to set the sole of her foot on the ground for delicateness," can find a path of duty over velvet carpets, and joy to tread it bearing her cross, while she is studying and praying for the best way, the fittest time, and the choicest words, in which to plead for Jesus.

> " Oh, the true cross can never rest
>   On shoulders light and vain,
> Or sparkle on a thoughtless breast,
>   Hung by a golden chain.
>
> ' Tis not a gem or amulet,
>   A charm by beauty worn ;
> But *toil* in self-*denial* set,
>   And daily up hill borne."

Where in this favored day are our Madame Guyons with hearts aglow, to move in the palaces of the noble, and write and talk with inspiring ardor of the love of our Redeemer?

INVITING TO CHRIST.

Perhaps there is no duty so self-deny‐ing, from which there is so much shrink‐ing, as *close personal religious conversation,* pressing the claims of Christ on those who neglect him.

Christians say to you, "We will do any other work: we cannot do this." Some will plead, "We are too inconsistent." Such should examine themselves, and see what is the sin which they think will rise before others or trouble their own consciences when they speak, and strive to put away that sin.

"But we cannot rebuke others, we cannot preach," they object. You need not do either: use gentle persuasion. "They will think us impertinent." No, indeed. They will be more likely to think you remiss if you neglect it. "I shall be repulsed." What matter? Christ was sometimes repulsed, yet he saved men. Try and see. They may say, "We have been hoping you would introduce this subject." Depend upon it, many are longing for this help, waiting, and wondering when some Christian will speak to them. Your interest for their souls may arouse them to feeling. The anxiety you manifest for them will represent to them the compassionate heart of Jesus. They will consider your words another call of God's mercy.

The refinement of feeling, which gives you a sense of the delicacy and difficulty of the work fits you for it, provided only, that, relying on the Saviour's strength, you undertake it.

The weak and irresolute, and those unfavorably situated, are often grateful for aid from a stronger will and firmer convictions than their own, and thank you for urging, "You will not let these things slip. Promise me that you will surely pray to-day." So to the timid, who shrink from acknowledged duties, you may say, " Next communion is the time: sun or rain, alone or with company, pray come out and confess Christ."

Christians who are so fearful of giving offence greatly misjudge the world around them.

A factory girl complained that she had worked four months in the same room with three professed Christians, and not one thought enough of her to inquire whether she had any interest in religion.

We asked a young lady visiting in town, " Is there not some one in your own home you can talk with to keep up your interest?" She answered bitterly, " No, indeed! Nobody in that church cares a straw whether I am converted." Why was it, Christian friends, that she knew so little of their hearts?

How often the unconverted say of us, " If they believed what they profess, they would show more concern for us " !

Were not the stubborn facts before us, we should not believe there could be such remissness. A woman moved into a neighboring village; and, after a year, not one of her many Christian neighbors knew whether she belonged to any church. Two women lived side by side, exchanging kindly calls, and talking freely about every other matter : and yet the professor never introduced the most important subject, or knew the spiritual condition of the non-professor. Alas, alas ! how willing to go to heaven alone, and wear a starless crown !

SUCCESSFUL LABORERS.

In contrast with all this, President

Finney in his tract, " Power from on
High," says, " Women have possessed
this power, and very often in a remarkable degree. Paul had his female helpers
in proclaiming the gospel, whose usefulness he was frank to acknowledge. In
every age of the Church, and especially
wherever revivals of religion have ex-
isted, this power has been given to wom-
en, as well as men. I am rejoiced to
know that the American Board is learn-
ing more and more the power and usefulness of female laborers in the missionary field. However men may interpret
the Bible, whatever prejudices may exist
in any branch of the Church against the
public gospel labors of females, the fact
remains, that God imparts to females,
often in an eminent degree, the power to
win souls to Christ. I have myself

known a goodly number of women, who have been among the most efficient laborers' for souls I could anywhere find. I could name women of diverse ages and culture, upon whom rested this power from on high, in a degree too manifest to be overlooked or denied."

Read the memoir of the faithful worker, Fidelia Fiske, and notice how many heathen girls she won to Christ. She was in a school, you say, and had great opportunities. Yes, she was surrounded by girls; but they were heathen girls, — lying, thieving, unchaste: yet she became the means of converting many of them to become devoted missionary women, true workers for Christ. Had we half her consecration and singleness of purpose, we might surely win some American girls. We may be obscure sisters, but the lives of all such women remind us, —

"We may make our lives sublime."

Every class of Christians should strive to act at least on their own class among the worldly. Pious girls should persuade other girls ; the old should exhort those of their own age. The laboring woman should tell another how Christ helps her to bear her burdens and to be contented with her lot. Those who are convinced that this speaking for Jesus is duty should urge it upon those who fail to do it.

About three years ago, forty members of one church, male and female, banded themselves together for Christian work. Each one selected two or three individuals from the surrounding community, and promised to pray earnestly and labor faithfully for their salvation. The result was that numerous conversions occurred constantly around them for three years. When questioned in regard to this long-continued work of grace, they all answered, "It was God's blessing upon work." Why cannot every church do something like this, — appoint persons to look after every one within its reach?

Dear friends, let us each ask ourselves to-day, Whom we are helping heavenward? Over whom are we exerting a blessed influence? What persons will we select, *this hour*, as subjects of prayer and labor, until they are entirely devoted to the Lord?

RICH REWARD.

Our blessed Lord bestows a direct and

precious reward upon all who truly work
for the Church.

If you study the history of his life,
you will marvel at his keen appreciation
and warm commendation of every service rendered by women. It was like
his thoughtful tenderness, for Paul to
send greeting to each of the sisters, by
name, who had worked for the early
Church. We almost hear his own loving
voice saying, " Salute the beloved Persis,
who labored much in the Lord."

In a letter just received from a missionary in Africa, she writes, "When
Major Malan was here, he broke out in
a kind of rapturous delight one day, as
he said, ' Did you ever feel greater joy
at any thing than the privilege of open-
ing the way of salvation to a sinner
who does not care for himself, but you
long to have him saved? What can

equal it?' I have often thought," she continues, " of the intense joy he seemed to feel at the remembrance of such op tunities. And how happy we might *all* be, if we would thus earnestly work for Jesus ! "

Notice, dear sisters, it is not *success* that is rewarded, but the *effort.* The results we leave meekly with God; the happiness in doing the work is our own.

Every one who has faithfully preached Christ, written lovingly of him to win souls to him, or with a full heart ex- horted sinners to receive him, can testify that there came into the heart a new love for Christ and for souls; and, as love and joy are inseparable, with the love came a great joy.

When you become fully engaged in this work, life can no longer be vacant and dull. You begin to live as the angels live; to feed on their food, and taste their delight. More than this, you come into sympathy with Christ in his redeeming work; you are exalted to be a co-worker with him. You may sometimes be a partaker of his sufferings, but you will also share the divine blessedness. His joy will remain with you, and your joy will be full.

When the artist Cole found he had painted a religious picture, he suddenly awoke to a consciousness of his own capabilities, and made a new life purpose. Often it is the new purpose and new effort that show us our capabilities. May we now come up to his high resolve, when he exclaimed, "I am going to work for the Church, I am going to work for the Church!"